THE SUNDHYA

OR

THE DAILY PRAYERS

OF THE

BRAHMINS

THE SUNDHYA

OR

THE DAILY PRAYERS

OF THE

BRAHMINS

S.C BELNOS

GYAN

Published by

Gyan Publishing House
5, Ansari Road
Daryaganj, New Delhi-110002
Phone: 011-47034999, 9811692060
E-mail: books@gyanbooks.com

Distribution Network
gyanbooks.com
India, USA, Canada, UK, Australia

ISBN: 978-93-6433-038-1 (HB)

First Published, 1851

2nd Impression 2024

Printed at: Gyan Press, Delhi.

THE SUNDHYA OR THE DAILY PRAYERS OF THE BRAHMINS
Author: S.C BELNOS

THE SUNDHYA

OR

THE DAILY PRAYERS

OF THE

Brahmins.

ILLUSTRATED

IN

A SERIES OF ORIGINAL DRAWINGS FROM NATURE, DEMONSTRATING THEIR ATTITUDES AND DIFFERENT SIGNS AND FIGURES PERFORMED BY THEM DURING THE CEREMONIES OF THEIR MORNING DEVOTIONS, AND LIKEWISE THEIR POOJAS.

TOGETHER WITH

ALLAHBAD.

[illegible] Junction of the Ganges and the Jumna. — in the bed of the river is a [illegible] well called [illegible]

A DESCRIPTIVE TEXT ANNEXED TO EACH PLATE, AND THE PRAYERS FROM THE SANSCRIT, TRANSLATED INTO ENGLISH

IN

TWENTY FOUR PLATES

BY

Mrs S. C. Belnos.

1851.

INTRODUCTORY PREFACE.

Shortly after my residence in Bengal, my observation was attracted to the many interesting novelties which the habits and manners of the Natives exhibited; and of a few of which I have attempted, in a former work, to offer some illustration. There remained, however, various singular practices connected with their religious system which appeared to me to deserve more careful attention, forming, as they evidently did, an essential element in the daily rituals of the Hindoos, and particularly of the Brahmans.

Upon endeavouring to obtain some precise information regarding these practices, I found that, although various useful publications contained a general description of the Brahmanical ceremonies, and in particular of the Sundhya, or the daily recitals of prayers accompanied with certain gesticulations, I found that mere general description was inadequate to convey an exact notion of the practices which were daily and hourly exhibited on the banks of the Ganges by Hindoo devotees, and that pictorial illustration was indispensably necessary to represent, in an intelligible manner, their actual performance. I therefore resolved to engage in the accomplishment of a task which had hitherto been unattempted, and offer to the public a faithful representation of some of the objects which are most striking to the European traveller as he passes by the landing-places attached to villages and towns along the sandy banks of the rivers of India: at the same time, I determined to ascertain as far as was possible, by one not professing any conversancy with oriental lore beyond the familiar use of the spoken language, the purpose and object of the ceremonial, so as to render the representations the means of conveying some information which might contribute to the better understanding of the notions and practices of the numerous and interesting races of India, which, notwithstanding their differences of creed and complexion, are subjects of the British Crown.

Upon commencing my task, however, I found that I had to encounter difficulties as serious as unexpected, as a mere general sketch of the attitudes and gesticulations of the Brahmans at the season of worship, however graphic, could not express that minute accuracy which it was my great desire faithfully to preserve. It was necessary that the worshipper should deliberately perform his exercises in my presence, so as to afford me time and opportunity to delineate them with precision. That there should have been much reluctance in complying with this requisition was not unnatural, as it was asking the performer to exhibit rites considered by him as solemn and sacred, for a secular and profane purpose; but this natural reluctance became inflexible refusal on the part of the Brahmans of Bengal, none of whom would consent to perform those rites in my presence, or impart to a female, and an impure European, any of the mysteries of their religion. I was therefore unable to make any progress whilst I resided in Calcutta, and awaited the prospect of a visit to the Upper Provinces, and to the Holy City of Benares (the chief seat of Brahmanical learning), where I was led to expect I should meet with individuals less bigoted and intolerant than the Brahmans of Bengal.

Accordingly, as soon as opportunity admitted, and I was settled for some time at Benares, I set on foot an inquiry for such an informant as was required for my investigations. It was not easy to meet with one, as few Brahmans would condescend to enlighten a European female on such grave topics; nor could they comprehend why I should feel any interest in the subject, or take any pains for a purpose (which they considered) so incompatible with my sex and *caste*. I was not discouraged, however; and by unremitting perseverance, and by liberal remunerations, I at length prevailed on a Brahman, who professed to be acquainted with Sanscrit literature, and who officiated as a Priest in one of the Temples of Benares, to go through all the ceremonial of his daily worship in my presence, and to furnish me with the prayers used on these occasions. Accordingly, I delineated the positions through which he went in the course of his adorations with the most careful exactness, and translated, from his explanations in the vernacular Hindoostani, the names and attributes of the Deities addressed, and the prayers by which they were propitiated. I also received from the Pundit copies of the original texts, which I have submitted to the perusal of Professor WILSON, who has expressed himself satisfied with their general authenticity and correctness, but has not considered them to be sufficiently accurate for publication; as the Pundit, although possessed of the average popular attainments of the class to which he belonged, and thoroughly master of the practices of his religion, was evidently not a profound Sanscrit scholar. The translations which I made have been also revised by the same Gentleman, and are considered by him to convey an accurate expression of the sense and purport of the originals.

In undertaking to delineate and describe this portion of the religious ceremonies of the Hindoos I have not intended to do more than communicate a correct idea of the practices which are obvious to the daily observer, and not to enter into the recondite subject of the religion itself. It must be sufficiently apparent that the observances which it authorises are of the most puerile and absurd nature; but they are not the less deserving of notice, when we find them taking a firm hold of the minds of otherwise intelligent individuals, and exercising so much influence over their belief and conduct. For however absurd, and, to Europeans, ridiculous, these practices may appear; however unmeaning the prayers and stanzas which are repeated may be; yet there is no doubt that the Brahmans are in earnest in performing the one and reciting the other, from the unmoved gravity of demeanour and the solemn tone in which the mysterious Slokas are repeated; imparting to the whole an air of solemnity strangely at variance with the frivolous gesticulations and empty repetitions by which they are accompanied, and which are so unworthy of rational and intellectual beings, the performance of all which, there is reason to believe, is unsanctioned by their oldest and most weighty authorities, and have sprung up, in comparatively recent times, from a corrupted and questionable source. At any rate the more precise and accurate the knowledge which Europeans acquire of the deformities and absurdities of the Hindoo religion, the more competent will they be to contend with those by whom they are held in mistaken veneration, to convince them of their errors, and ultimately lead them to the adoption of a purer and more holy faith.

Although I had no reason to doubt that the Pundit whom I had employed was fully capable of giving me the information I required; yet, having had ample experience of the native character to know that implicit reliance is not to be placed upon any Native of India, I took every opportunity I could of verifying the fidelity of my representations; and in the course of a tour to Mathura, Goverddhun, and Budrabinn, all places of great holiness in the eyes of the Hindoos of the Vaishnava sects, and the residence and resort of numerous religious characters, I exhibited my drawings to several Brahmans and ascetics. They all expressed the greatest surprise—and some no little indignation—at my being in possession of such particulars; but they admitted, without exception, their truth and accuracy. I placed the drawings also before several eminent Oriental scholars in India, who likewise expressed their entire conviction of their correctness. I may add to this the testimony of the most competent judges in this country; and I may therefore venture to claim the merit of truthfulness, at least, for the work which I now offer to the public, as an humble contribution to that elucidation of the religion and the manners of the Hindoos, which has been thought worthy of the talents of so many eminent scholars, both in India and in Europe.

April 1851.

PLATE I.

THE BRAHMIN'S FIRST MORNING PRAYER TO THE GOOROO ON RISING.

It is habitual with the Natives, all over India, to rise with the first dawn of day. The Brahmin sits up on his charpaya or on a mat on the ground, and, joining his hands, repeats the following prayer to the Gooroo (High Priest), who is considered by the Hindoos to be invested with the power of a Deity, and to have sprung from the Gods. To him the Brahmin offers up his first morning orisons. The words, in Sanscrit, are as contained in the Poorans, the following being a literal translation:—

"I glorify thee, Benign, who rests upon a serpent, from whose navel the lotus springs; God of Gods! the supporter of the universe; beautiful as the azure of the sky; cloud-like in colour; elegant in form.

"The husband of Luxshmee, lotus-eyed, worthy the contemplation of sages! Vishnoo, the preserver and destroyer of the world! the only Lord of the universe!

"I glorify him who is to be always contemplated, the remover of all stains, the granter of all desires, the essence of all holy shrines; who is praised by Siva and by Brahma, the universal refuge, the assuager of the pain of his servants, the protector of those who bend before him, the bark to bear us over the ocean of the world. I praise thy lotus-feet, oh mighty Male."

श्रीगणेशायनमः अथध्यानस्यश्लोकोयंलिख्यते

शांताकारंभुजगशयनं पद्मनाभंसुरेशं विश्वाधारंगगनसदृशंमेघवर्णंशुभांगं ।

लक्ष्मीकांतंकमलनयनंयोगिभिर्ध्यानगम्यं वंदेविष्णुंभवभयहरंसर्वलोकैकनाथं ॥ १ ॥

अथप्रणामस्यश्लोकोयंलिख्यते

ध्येयंसदापरिभवघ्नमभीष्टदोहं तीर्थास्पदंशिवविरिंचिनुतंशरण्यं ।

भृत्यार्तिहं प्रणतपालं भवाब्धिपोतं वंदेमहापुरुषतेचरणारविंदं ॥ २ ॥

PLATE I

THE BRAHMINS FIRST PRAYER TO THE GURDO

PLATE 2.

THE BRAHMIN'S FIRST CEREMONY ON ENTERING THE GANGES.

He repeats the Gungashtuk.

Having terminated his prayers to the Gooroo, he quits his place of repose; and filling a brass vessel, called Julpatree, he commences by washing his face and rubbing his teeth, praying at the same time, that all impurity may thus be cleansed away from him, and he be made as pure within as without. Then, proceeding to the river-side, he enters the Ganges, knee-deep, sprinkles a little water, by a quick jerk of the right-hand, over his head; and holding some in the half-closed palm of the same hand, he addresses the great Deity Bhagwan in the following words:—

"Vishnu! Vishnu! Vishnu! Adoration to the supreme Deity! the first eternal male! the resplendent sun! May the benefits that result from this adoration be bestowed (on such a person—naming himself) performing worship in Jambu Dwípa (India) in the second portion of the life of Brahma, in the Kalpa of Varáha, in the Manwantara (or reign of the Manu) Vaivaswata, at this holy spot on (such) a year (such) a fortnight, when the sun was in an auspicious sign! for I am desirous of fulfilling the duties which are enjoined by the Purans, the Smriti (law), and the Srutí (or Vedas)."

This said, he plunges several times in the Ganges; and while he rubs each member of his body in the sacred stream, he chants the following verses in praise of Gunga:—

1st verse. "When a man goes into the sacred waters, he must sing her praise thus: 'O Juggutmata! whoever shall, day and night, fix his heart and his thoughts upon thee, is righteous and holy in all his works; and he who worships thee, in the hope of obtaining a place in heaven, will not be disappointed. O Mata! (mother) all my hopes of salvation are in thy hands! Grant me every good in this life, and heaven in the one to come!'

2d verse. "Those whom thou hast endowed with handsome features, and full, lovely eyes, their beauty is consecrated to thy service, that they might gaze upon thee with admiration and adoration. O Mata! he whose hearing is deaf to the rippling of thy waters, is worthless in thy sight.

3d verse. "O Gunga! the gods descend in their glorious cars, to bathe in thy holy stream! The sinner, who hath been condemned to the regions of darkness and punishment, by washing in thy sacred water shall be purified, and received in the realms of everlasting bliss. Blessed is the land through which thou flowest, for thou deliverest the people thereof from all sorrow and evils; and gods adore thee!

4th verse. "He who strikes a Priest, commits robbery, seduces the wife of his teacher, and he who is given to drunkenness; yea, even he who hath committed all these crimes, if, when brought dying to thy sacred waters, he shall drink thereof, he shall surely see heaven.

5th verse. "O Mata! all the rivers in the world take their source from thee, O Junani! those even who are suffering in purgatory thou canst, by thy grace, convey at once to heaven.

6th verse. "Whoever bathes, swims, plays, and enjoys himself in thy beautiful stream, were he to deny the power of all other gods, and even of purgatory, and adored only thee, still will he be sanctified, and received in the realms of joy everlasting.

7th verse. "He who gives unto the poor in this life, and is righteous in all his works, and contemplates holy things, by bathing in thy waters, shall go direct to heaven; as also those who praise thee, and present thee offerings.

8th verse. "The elephant, horse, camel, rats, mice, and the musk-deer, O Mata! even these, by drinking of thy waters, become greater than the gods. The Rajah and the Brahmin, that neglect thy worship, are reputed only as the lowest caste of mankind.

9th verse. "O Mata! those who live daily in iniquity, and spread devastation over the world; and those that are insane, uncharitable, unrighteous, and commit every species of crime; should, in the hour of death, cry 'O Gunga!' three times, and shall find salvation, and go to heaven.

10th. verse. "O Gunga! (my father) Bhawaneedass is thy servant: keep him in prosperity and happiness; and give sons unto (my brother) Nityanund! O Mata! preserve (my son) Ramrutna from all sickness and other ills of this life; and we shall ever worship thy sacred stream."

Hindoo devotees repeat these and other long verses; but the above number is considered, generally, sufficient during ablutions. The Gungashtuks, or praises of the Ganges, are not particularly confined to the sacred books; but are supposed to be the inspirations of certain holy sages, or Rishis.

PLATE 2

GUNGASHTUK

PLATE 3.

THE purification by frequent immersion in the sacred stream being completed, the Brahmin changes his dhotee (wrapping garment) for a dry, coloured one; either red, yellow, or orange. These colours are worn principally by the Hindoos of the Upper Provinces. He spreads a small mat upon a dry spot on the banks of the river; and seating himself cross-legged, the right lying on the left, which posture he retains immovably for two or three hours together, he performs with his hands and fingers all the ceremonies of the morning devotions to the Deities, commencing with the principal ones; as Mahadeo, Vishnoo, &c. The various figures executed with the hands and fingers are performed with wonderful rapidity, the votary repeating at the same time the names of each figure; as Ek Mookhum, Do Mookhum, Teen Mookhum, Choutah Mookhum. As there is no variety in the position of the body as far as twenty-one moodras, I have merely illustrated the hands and fingers. No. 3, being the fixed one, is called the koorma (tortoise): it counts for one moodra. Plates 6, 7, and 8, are also moodras; but the position is altered.

PLATE 3

KOORMA (TORTOISE)

PLATES 4 & 5.

No other meaning is attached to these figures, but that they are pleasing to the Deities. The Brahmin commences with the figure No. 1, Soon-mookum (the closed lotus); then gradually spreading his fingers, describes the full-blown flower. He then makes the sign of Ek-mookum, Do-mookum, Teen-mookum, Choutah-mookum, and then the rest of the figures illustrated in Plates 4, 5, 6, 7, and 8. These are called Moodras, of which there are twenty-four in the Sundhya.

PLATE 4

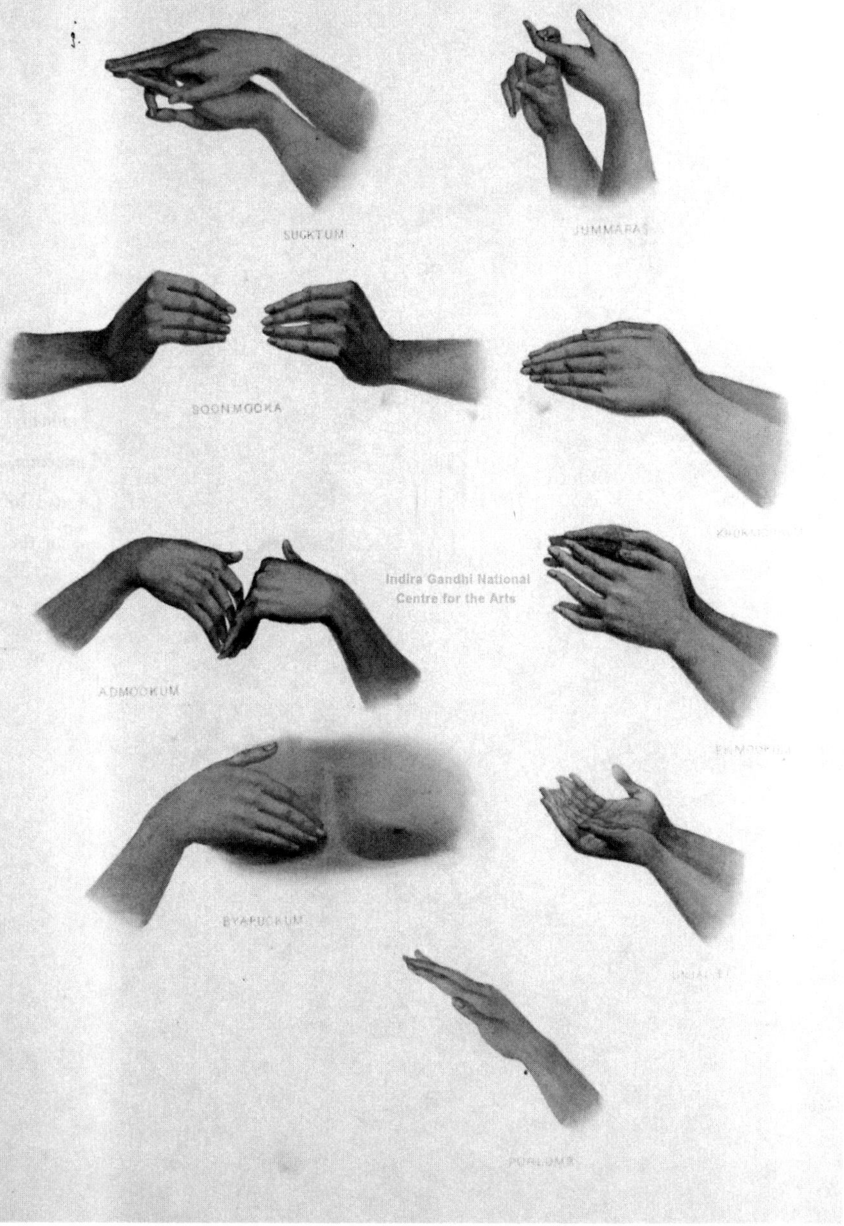

PLATE 5

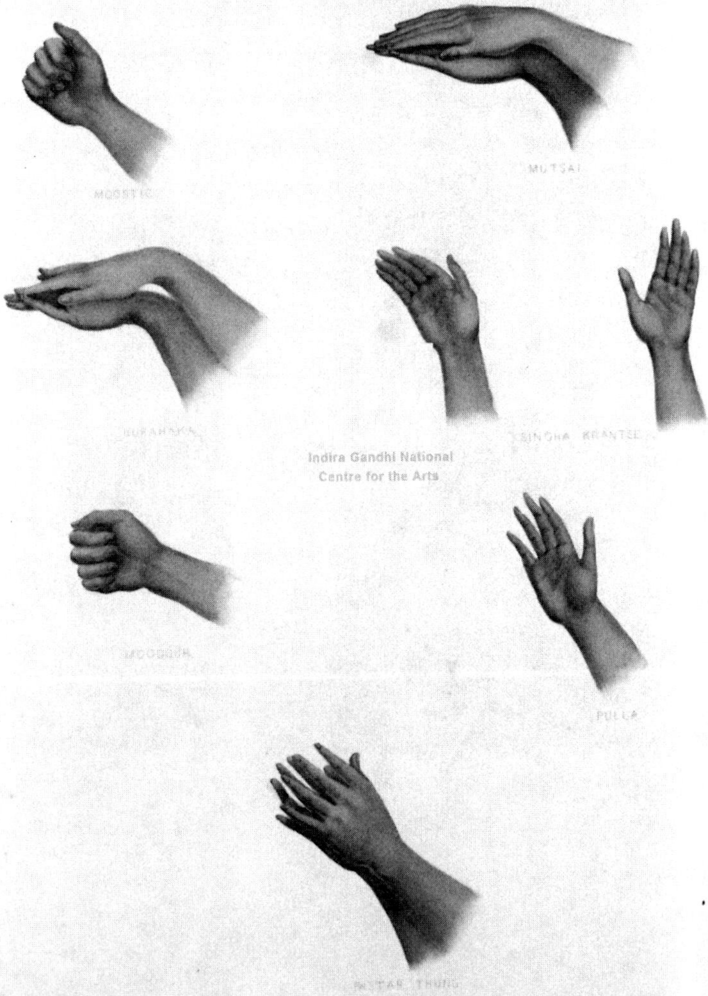

PLATE 6.

After having performed all the figures contained in Plates 4 and 5, the Brahmin proceeds to the Pranayama, taking an inward view of Vishnoo Bhagwan, and Mahadeo; the first, "Preserver of the Universe," the latter, "The Destroyer of all." This ceremony is performed in the following manner: 1st, he presses in the right nostril with the fourth finger of his left hand, repeating the name of each Deity; and counting them nine times over upon the joints of the fingers of his right hand with great rapidity, half closing his eyes the while, and drawing in his breath: then gently pressing in the left nostril with the thumb, as in fig. 2, he breathes out, repeating the same name as many times over. Then releasing the right nostril, and still pressing in the left with the thumb, as in fig. 3, he terminates the Pranayama. These names, &c., are not uttered aloud, but merely by the movement of the lips.

PLATE 6.

No. 2, KUMBUCK

No. 3, RAICHUCK

No. 1, POORUCK PRANAIYAM

PLATE 7.

THE Pranayama concluded, the Brahmin takes up water in the palm of his left hand; and, touching it with the tips of the fingers of his right hand, he sprinkles it over his head. Then, dropping his right hand, and taking up fresh water, he presents it to the right nostril, drawing in his breath; then pours out the water on the left side of the palm. He then takes up the Urgha (a long, shallow vessel of copper), filled with water, over which he strews yellow and red sandal, raw rice, and a few flowers (the Hindoos are not particular in the choice of the flowers in these prayers): then, rising from his seat, he holds the Urgha with both hands, passing one end of the Janeo (Brahminic thread) over the thumb and the Urgha, and repeating the following prayer to the sun:—

अथार्घ्यमंत्रःसूर्य्यस्यकथ्यते

एहि सूर्यसहस्रांशो तेजोराशे जगत्पते अनुकंपयमां भक्त्या गृहाणार्घ्यं दिवाकर

TRANSLATION.

Oh, Sun of a thousand rays! most glorious Lord of the world! have mercy upon me! I am thy servant: accept my offering of water, oh, Lord of the day!

Here the Brahmin pours out the contents of the Urgha.

PLATE 7.

URCHAI, OFFERING OF WATER, RICE, &c. &c.

Day & Son, Lith^rs to The Queen.

PLATE 8.

He then makes the sign, as illustrated in this Plate, with the hands and fingers, forming a hole between the middle fingers: holding them up to his left eye, he takes a survey of the sun. After this he resumes his seat, in the same attitude as before, the right leg crossed over the left, and then proceeds to the Gáyatri-Jup.

अथनमस्कारमंत्रःसूर्य्यस्य

आदित्यंये नमस्कारं प्रकुर्वंति दिनेदिने जन्मांतरसहस्रेषु दारिद्र्यं नोपजायते।

Translation.

"Whatever mortals in this world offer thee thanksgiving day by day, will never experience poverty in a thousand births."

PLATE 8.

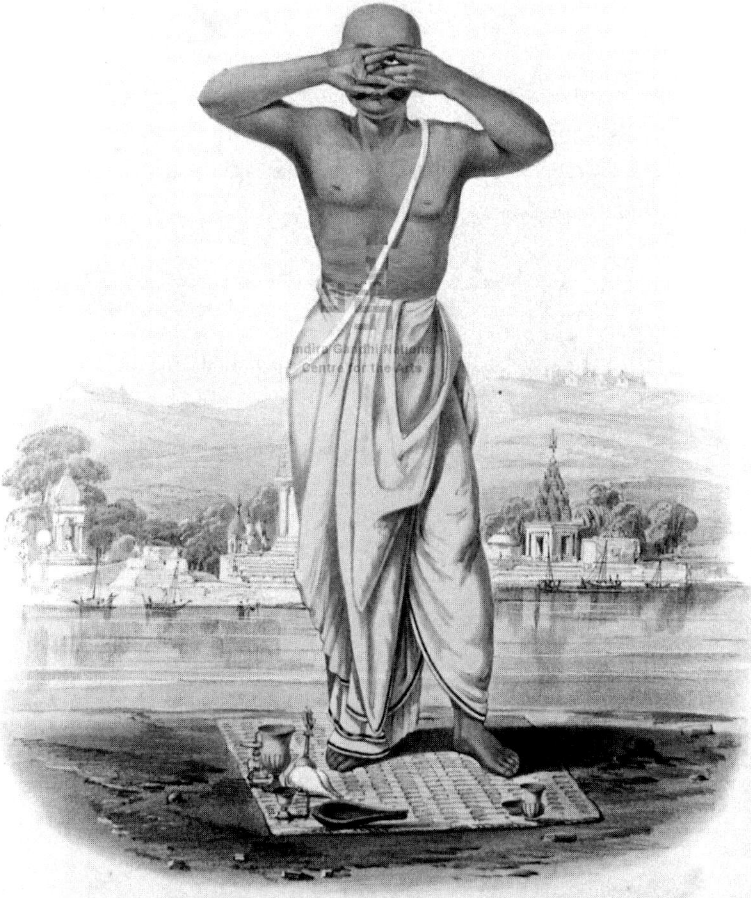

SOORYA

PLATE 9.

THIS prayer is called the Gáyatri-Jup: it is secret, and cannot be divulged to any but a Brahmin: it must be whispered only in his ear. The figures performed with the right hand, while the left one hangs listlessly over his right foot, must be cautiously concealed from all prying eyes by a red cloth bag, drawn over the hand, and hanging down on all sides. This bag is called Gumookhi, and is generally made of red broad-cloth. The Hindoos, however, commonly content themselves with throwing a part of their wrapping-cloth over the hand, which serves the same purpose as the bag.

PLATE 9[illegible]

GAYATRI JUP.

THE SECRET PRAYER.

PLATE 10.

After the secret prayer, he makes the sign of the eight Moodras, six of which are illustrated in the Plate. The remainder, *i.e.* Gyan and Bairagya, I have given in the two following Plates.

PLATE 10

SIGNS OF THE GUYATRI

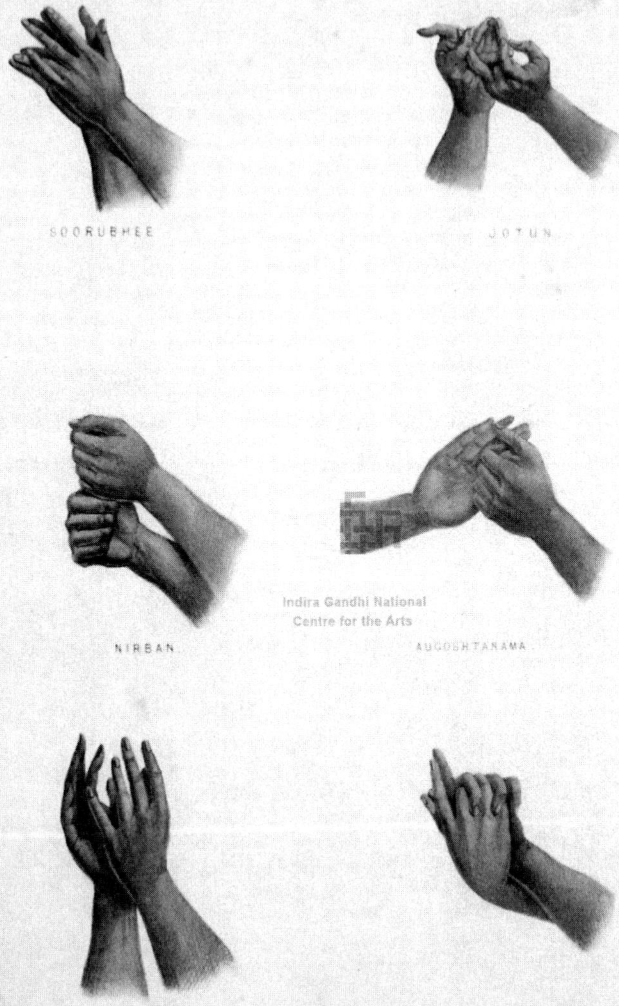

PLATE II.

As the two remaining figures of the eight Moodras in the "Gáyatri-Jup" are performed by a change of posture, I have given the full figure of the praying devotee; the right arm resting over the knee of his right leg, the great toe of which foot he holds with the thumb and index.

PLATE 8.

G Y A N

PLATE 12.

This concludes the ceremony performed by the Brahmins daily in their sacred stream, or on the banks of the river. The generality of the Hindoos, however, do not adhere strictly to the performance of every part of the ceremonies enjoined by their Poorans and Shasters, but merely repeating the first few Moodras, and then, sprinkling some water on the head, they go home. It is all a matter of conscience with the inferior sects of Hindoos whether they perform the ceremonies prescribed by their religion strictly, or otherwise; these consisting generally of the working classes and men of business, who are forced to shorten their devotion from press of time, and various other causes.

PLATE 12

BHYRAGAI

PLATES 13 & 14.

THESE vessels are indispensable in all their religious ceremonies, and are 16 in number, viz.

Shunkh.—The conch-shell.

Artee is borne by the figure of Balgovind, an attendant on the Gods: he holds five brass lamps, which are lighted in particular ceremonies. The Devotee gives it a circular movement as he holds it up before the image of the Deity worshipped, so as to throw the rays of the light equally on every part.

Ghunta.—(Bell). The figure on the top represents one of their angels. The bell is rung when the conch is blown: this is done to call the attention of the Gods.

Urgha.—A copper vessel used in the ablutions of the images.

Dhoopdan.—For burning incense before the image.

Abkhora.—A ewer for presenting drink-offerings to the Gods.

Nundee.—The humped bull on which Mahadeo rides.

Sumputnee.—A copper vessel used also in presenting offerings.

Kuttoree.—Also of copper, to give offerings of flowers.

Thalee.—A large brass round dish for offering fruits and sweetmeats.

Dhoopdanee.—A smaller brass vessel for offering incense.

Laghupatra.—A small brass cup to mix up sandal in.

Singhasan.—The chair or seat for the images or idols.

Brihut Achamani.—A large spoon, to offer water to the Deity.

Laghu Achamani.—To offer water to the Deity, to cleanse his mouth.

Shunkh (upon the stand "Tictee") is used to pour water upon the idols.

PLATE 13

ARTEE PUNCH PURDEEP
GHUNTA
NUNDEE
SHUNKH TAIRUTREE
DHOOPDAN
UPKHORA
URGHA
SHUNKH

PLATE 14

DHOOPDAN
SAMPUTEE
KUTTORA
SINGHASUN
THALEE
LUGHU ACHMANEE
ACHMANEE

PLATE 15.

POOJA OF VISHNOO--POURING WATER UPON THE SALIGRAM.

The Saligram is a small red stone, a kind of Ammonite, found in the River Gunduck; and is held sacred by the Hindoos, and worshipped as an Idol. According to the Poorans, it is dedicated to Vishnoo: it is kept in a small box of any white metal the worshipper may have the means of procuring: iron alone is excluded. The Artee, Dhoopdanee, Thalee, Ghunta, Abkhora, Sumputtee Kuttoree, red and yellow sandal-flowers, toolsee, betel-leaves, sooparee, areka-nut, jeneo, a piece of cloth to cover the Saligram, sweetmeats, and the shunk, or conch shell, are all necessary in this worship. From this deity the votary supplicates never to be born again in this world. This sign  is worn, on the forehead between the eyebrow, and is put on in the Pooja of Vishnoo: it is done with the mud of the sacred stream: many draw it on the breast and arms also. The necklace is of toolsee-seeds.

Translation from the Sanskrit Verses in the Pooja of Vishnoo.

SALIGRAM, THE TYPE OF VISHNOO.

Invocation to the Deity.

1st verse. O Deo! O Bhagwan! O Purmeswur! transfer thy omnipotent presence from the realms of ether, and descend to the region of mortals. Approach, O sovereign Deity! Behold, I lay before thee my thank-offerings, that thou mayest at all times be pleased with my works.

2d verse. (Placing the Idol upon the Singhasun, he proceeds)—O Prubhoo! behold, thy chair is made of the purest gold, and it is studded with the most precious gems, and the shape thereof is like unto a lion. Sit thou upon thy throne, even as the earth, which the great serpent Shes-nág bears, is thy footstool.

3d verse. O Deva! behold, for thy ablution I have prepared the water warmed and perfumed with a thousand odoriferous flowers. Accept it, and bathe: and be merciful to thy servant.

7th verse. O Vishnoo! behold, here is raiment for thee, for winter and for summer, of the finest texture, and of costly materials; so that thou being well clothed, thy countenance will shine in beatitude.

8th verse. O Deva! this Jeneo is the one which Brahma hath woven with thread, and the knot of Vishnoo is upon it. O Junardun, accept my offering.

9th verse. O Deva! Malayachali's (sandal), when applied to the breast and brow, gives internal delight; such sandal accept thou from my hands.

10th verse. O Vishnoo! these flowers which I strew before thy image are of various colours and kinds, and are all of the season: may they be acceptable to thee.

11th verse. O Deo! I offer up burnt incense unto thee, extracted from aromatic plants and flowers, and perfumes of many kinds: may it be pleasing and acceptable to thee.

12th verse. Behold! I dip this wick in melted butter, and this in camphor; which, with thy grace, will light the three worlds.

13th verse. O Deity! the repast I here lay before thy mighty presence is of the choicest ingredients, and is composed of four dishes cooked in various ways. Bhoksh (is made of milk and rice, and hulwa): Bhog (composed of poora pooree, chapatee, dall, and vegetable curry): Shookt (pickles and preserves): Ledge (sweetmeats): and Shut-rus (composed of six different relishes, *i. e.* salt, sweet, sour, pungent, bitter, and astringent, all mixed together). Such a repast is worthy of the Gods. Accept it at my hands.

14th verse. O Vishnoo! I offer thee these Bel-leaves: they are those which creep and twine round the Nagurbat. And behold! I put over them, areka-nut, nutmeg, cloves, cardemoms, which add to the aromatic scent and flavour of the Pan (betel-leaf). Accept it.

15th verse. O Deo! I walk round thy image seven times; and all that hath been enjoined by our holy writs for the performance of ceremonies I have done, and offered unto thee in this Pooja. Fulfil all its purpose!

16th verse. (Joining his hands before the Idol, he continues)—O Deva, I am a great sinner! I prostrate myself before thee! Have mercy upon me. I have strictly followed all the ordinances of my Religion; but nothing can avail without thy persevering mercies. I am floating upon the ocean of this world. Oh! bear me over in safety to the next.

17th verse. I have worshipped thee, but it is nought: I have performed all thy rites and ceremonies but without thy saving grace; all is in vain.

18th verse. O Sureswer! I have fully performed thy Poojah. Sanctify me.

19th verse. O Purumeswer! I, who am a poor ignorant mortal, forgive all my sins!

PLATE 5

POOJAH OF VISHNOO.

POURING WATER ON THE SALIGRAM

POOJA OF MAHADEO (MAHADEVA).

In the worship of this Deity the devotee requests grandeur and wealth. The horn of the deer is blown in this Pooja: offerings of fruit and sweetmeats are laid upon the Nundee; also the leaves of the bale-fruit tree, white flowers, a few blades of the dhoop-ghas (hay). The jeneo (brahmin-thread) is rolled up with areeka-nut and betel-leaves. The sign worn in this Pooja of Mahadeo is this , drawn with yellow sandal. The head, neck, and wrist are adorned with strings of the Roodrakh (the dried berries of the Eleocarpus).

Translation of the Version in the Pooja of Mahadeo.

1st verse. "O Earth! all the created beings who inhabit thee! and Devee, whom Vishnoo hath brought up from below! I likewise am thy inhabitant: sanctify me."

(Here the devotee takes up water in the palm of his right hand. After repeating the foregoing lines he sprinkles it under the mat upon which he is seated, puts some drops into his mouth, and, filling his half-closed palm with fresh water, says)—

2d verse. "O Shiu! fulfil the object of this my worship to thee. Give unto me all that my heart desireth, and deliver me from evil."

(He here pours out the water from his hand).

Muntra.

"Om Hrang, Hring, Hrong, Shivaya-nama."

(Then raising his joined hands to his head reverentially to the Deity, he spreads out his hands and fingers, which he slides down his whole figure from head to foot, and then makes the signs of the Kurna-nyas, after which the signs of the Hridayadi-nyas; then closing his eyes and folding his arms he proceeds to an inward contemplation of the gods, saying)—

1st verse. "I worship thee, Shiu! Thou art perpetually in my thoughts. Thou shinest like polished silver; and refulgent as the moon are thine ear-rings, and thy form appears resplendent with bright and precious jewels. In one hand thou bearest an axe, and in the other the skin of the deer. Thou sittest, with thy feet under thee, upon thy throne; and all the gods praise thee.

2d verse. "Thy covering is of the lion's skin; and thou art the first Male. Thou art the type of the world; and thou deliverest mankind from fear and danger. Thou hast five faces. Such art thou, Shiu. Reverence be unto thee.

3d verse. "Thou art light as the purest camphor. Thy mercies are infinite. The first and the last in the universe. Thy necklace is of entwined serpents. Such is Shiu: the Shiu who has Parbutee seated beside him. Reverence be to him."

(The devotee here makes a rough image, of mud, of Mahadeo, and places it upon the singhasun; then throws over it some grains of raw rice, and white flowers of dhatoora, saying)—

4th verse. "O Soopan, approach! O Pinakadhur, be thou seated here!"

(Then putting in the urgha some raw rice, flowers, and sandal, and holding it between his hands, he stands up before the idol).

5th verse. "From three dreadful diseases thou art the deliverer; and thou bestowest happiness on mankind. Receive my offerings, and preserve me from these three afflictions. Be merciful to my sons and daughters; and may they find grace before thee, O Bhooswamin."

(He pours out the contents of the urgha upon the image; then, dipping his fourth finger in honey, he touches the image: then, sprinkling the water over it, he performs the ceremony of ablution upon the idol. First he pours curds over it, then water, then melted butter (ghee), then water, then honey; water again, then milk; and finally, the five things together, and then washes out the whole with pure water. He then dresses the idol, and wraps an additional covering round it; and, throwing the jeneo over its shoulders, says)—

"The Yagnopaveet (the brahmanic thread) is a sign of holiness: it was brought from the heart of Brahma. He who wears it lives to a great age. Put away, then, all other works, O man! and invest thy body with the jeneo, for it bringeth light and strength."

(He then presents sandal, raw rice, areka-nuts, and the flowers thereof). "Thou art fruit in thyself; and thou bringest forth good fruit in them that worship thee. Thou art born of the genius Brihasput."

(He offers the sooparee (areka-nuts), and the flowers and leaves of the bale-tree; then the artee of eleven lamps. He next places sweetmeats before the image; then pours out some water before it. Laying down some leaves of betel, and some coins, he takes up rice in one hand, whilst with the other he throws a few grains upon the image, from time to time repeating the following):

"Aghor, I offer thee this! Pusooput, receive this! Bhyrav, I present thee this! Kupurdee, accept this! Isa, I offer thee this! Maheswar, accept my offering!"

(Then taking up more rice he says)—

"O thou who art in thyself earth, water, fire, wind, and the firmament, accept my offerings, and be merciful unto me! Shiva and Parbutee, have mercy upon me, and preserve me from all the evils of this life!"

(Joining his hands in supplication, he says)—

"Manifold are my sins; and I am ignorant of thy true worship. Neither do I know how to invoke thee, nor to sing thy praise, nor any single form of thy worship. As such have mercy upon me, and forgive my sins.

"He who shall chaunt thy praise when the day dawns shall obtain forgiveness for the sins of the past night. He who prays unto thee at mid-day, his sins, from his birth, shall be washed away; and he who worshippeth thee at the close of the day shall be purified from the sins of seven births. Even as the gift of five millions of milch-cows to as many Brahmins is propitious to the donor, and good in thy sight, so may this humble offering of thy servant find favour before thee."

(Then joining his hands again, he says)—

"O Hur, O Maheswar, O Sambhu, O Shiva, O Pusooput, Mahadeo, reverence be to thee!"

(Then taking up some raw rice and water in the palm of his hand he presents it to the image, concluding)—

"Accept this, O Deity; and give success to all my undertakings, and realize all the desires of my heart!"

PLATE 18.

POOJAH OF MAHADEO.

PLATES 17, 18, & 19.

POOJA TO DEVEE (SHIO SHIVA).

FROM Devee the Hindoo prays for the fulfilment of all his wishes. In this Pooja a book, called the Markundeya Pooran, is placed before him upon a red cloth, which serves as a case for the book when put by. A few blades of the dhoop ghas (hay), some red flowers, and sandal, rice, betel-leaves, and cloves, are placed upon the book, which remains closed. The worshipper sits cross-legged, the two heels and soles of the feet turned upwards, as illustrated in this Plate (a painful and difficult position); and with joined hands, having made his petition to the Deity, he performs the figures of the six Moodras contained in Plate 18, called Kurunnyas in the Gayatri: and then the Hridayadi'nyas, as in Plate 19. This ● is the sign worn in the worship of Devee between the two eyebrows, of red sandal: the Sputikmala, or string of crystal beads, is worn round the neck.

TRANSLATION OF THE VERSION IN THE DEVEE POOJA.

FROM THE MARKUNDEYA POORAN.

1st verse. "Markundeya saith, 'O Brahma! I beseech thee, instruct thy servant in that most secret prayer which will promote the welfare and happiness of mankind,' and by whom it was repeated.

2d verse. "Brahma answered and said, 'O Brahmin! O mighty Jogi! the secrets that I shall disclose unto thee for the salvation of man is the secret prayer to Devee, for she is holy. Hearken unto my words.'

3d verse. "Her titles are, Sylapootree[1], Brahmacharnee[2], Chundraghunta[3], Kokmunda[4], Scunda-Mata[5], Katyáyani[6], Kalaratree[7], Maha Gauri[8], Siddhada[9], Doorga[10]. These are her attributes: by these shalt thou do her worship.

6th verse. "He who shall offer her thanksgiving and praise, and worship her, shall surely be great.

7th verse. "Call ye upon these names in the field of battle, and ye shall surely conquer. Evil shall ever after flee from thee, and thou shalt be happy.

8th verse. "Chamunda mounts upon a corpse, Varáhee upon a buffalo; Aindri is seated upon an elephant, and Vaishnavee upon a pelican.

●

[1] Daughter of the hills.
[2] Virgin.
[3] Like the moon-bell.
[4] Pumpkin-faced.
[5] Mother of Scunda.
[6] Katyáyani.
[7] Midnight.
[8] Great Gauri, or fair complexioned.
[9] Granter of success.
[10] Difficult of access.

9th verse. "Maheswaree rides a bull; Kaumaree is seated upon a peacock.

10th verse. "The goddess Lukshmee upon a lotus. The flower thereof she taketh in her hand: the beloved of Vishnoo, fair and beautiful to look upon. Eeswaree is also mounted upon a bull.

11th verse. "Brahmee upon a swan, adorned in all her jewels of rare and brilliant gems.

12th verse. "And these goddesses, when filled with wrath, go forth, wielding these weapons:

13th verse. "Some the shunkh, some the discus, some the mace, some the spear, some the ploughshare, some the wooden pestle, some the club, some the javelin, some the axe, some the noose-rope, some the lance, some the trident, and some bows and arrows.

14th verse. "These they bear to slay the demons, for the protection of the good and the pious, and for the benefit of the gods.

15th verse. "(O disciples, join your hands in humble worship to Devee, and say), 'Glory to thee who art of mighty terror; possessed of fearful prowess, most strong, most energetic. The great remover of all fear; deliver me, O goddess, who art difficult to be seen, and strikest terror in all thy foes. May Aindri protect me in the east; may the god Agni protect me in the south-eastern region.' "

PLATE 17.

POOJA OF DEVEE-SHUCO, SHIVA

RUDMASHEEN.

PLATE 18

KURANYASA

IN THE GAYATRI-DEVEE POOJA

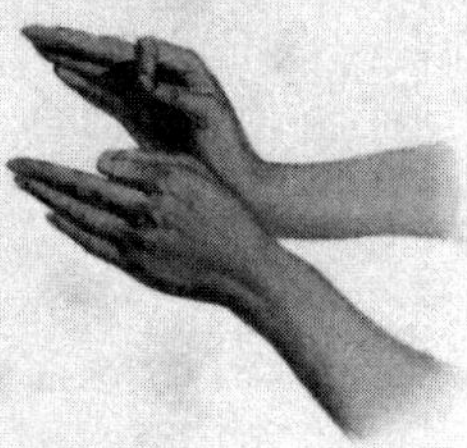

UNGOOSHTABHYAM NAMA

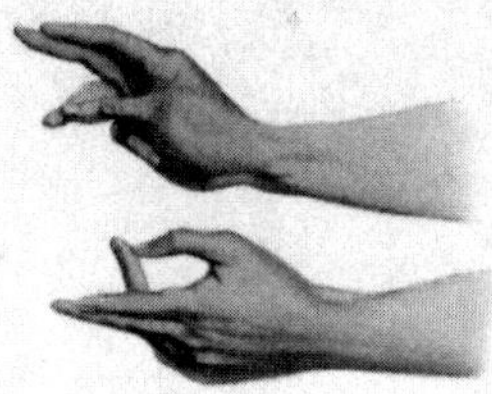

UNAMIKABHYAM NAMA

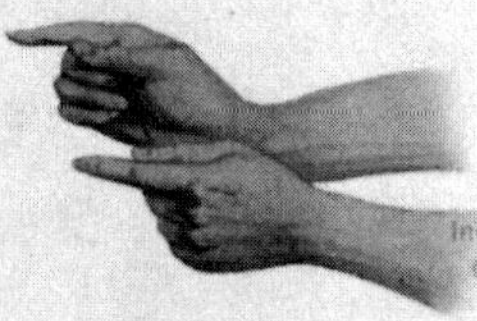

[illegible]JUNIBHYAM NAMA

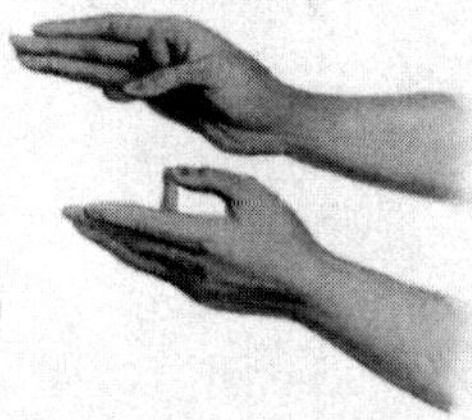

KUNISHTIKABHYAM NAMA

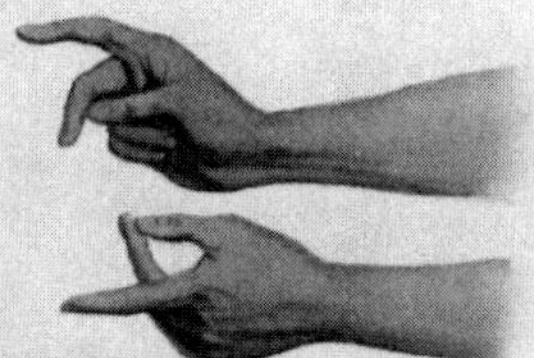

MUDHYMABHYAM NAMA

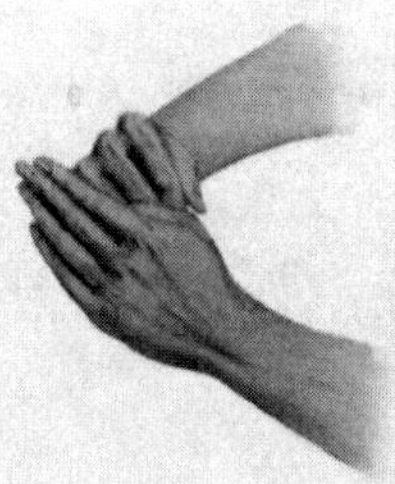

KURATALA-KURA-PRISHTA-BHYAM NAMA

PLATE 19

HRIDAYADI NYASA

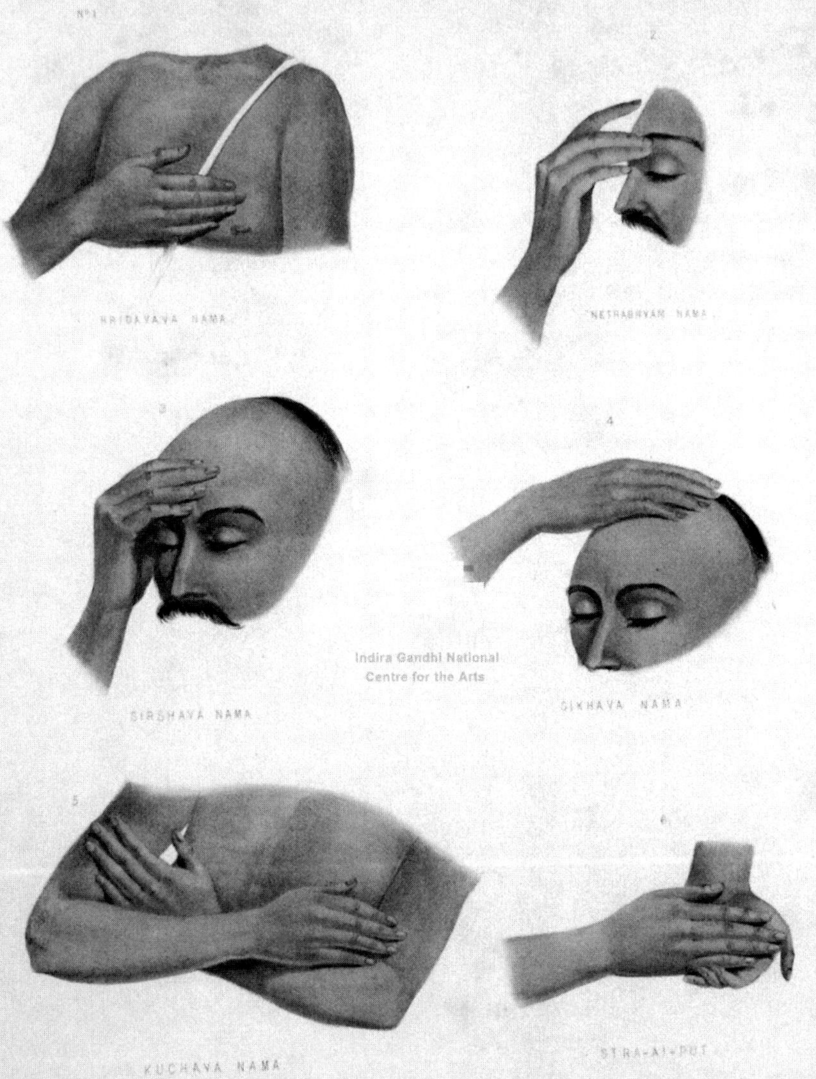

PLATE 20.

POOJA TO SOORYA (SUN).

The image of the sun, engraved on a silver plate, is placed in a Sumput (a wide copper vessel); raw rice, coloured with red sandal, some sandal, and red flowers, dhoop ghas, betel-leaves, areca-nut, red silk, the junes, dyed red, and all the brass vessels, images, &c., as daily used at their religious ceremonies. The Devotee stands upon one leg, the right foot against the left thigh, the heel turned outwards, and holding in his hands a brass cuttora (cup), containing a smaller one made of meal-dough, filled with ghee (melted butter), with a lighted wick placed in the middle. The sign worn in this Pooja is this ≡. The lines are drawn with sandal, and the spot in the middle with vermillion. A crystal necklace is also worn in this Poojah.

Translation of the Pooja of Soorya.

ORIGINAL VERSION FROM THE BHAVISHYOTTARA POORAN.

[*Presenting the Urgha, and joining his hands.*]

1st verse. "O thou of a thousand rays! O thou great, thou powerful luminary, supporter of the universe! I bow before thee, and worship thee with the Urgha: receive my offering, O god of light!

2d verse. "O Bhanu! thou who art immortal! the heavens, the earth, water, and fire, all proclaim and own thy power and greatness! Behold, I prostrate myself before thee, and present the offering of the Urgha! May it be acceptable to thee!

3d verse. "All that offer up thanksgiving to thee shall possess wealth and greatness, were his birth renewed a thousand times over!

4th verse. "Thou shinest upon the earth (in all the twelve months of the year) under the names of—

5th verse. "Aditya[1], Divakara[2], Bhaskar[3], Prabhakar[4], Huridaswa[5], Trailokya-lochana[6].

6th verse. "Mihira[7], Ravi[8], Dwijakara[9], Dwadsatmaka[10], Trimoortee[11], Soorya[12].

Sun presiding over

[1] March.	[7] September.
[2] April.	[8] October.
[3] May.	[9] November.
[4] June.	[10] December.
[5] July.	[11] January.
[6] August.	[12] February.

7th verse. "All who repeat these twelve names of the year, and present thee offerings, shall have happy dreams at night; and they shall be delivered from trouble and poverty.

8th verse. "Thou deliverest us from all the evils of the flesh, and from poverty. Even as the sacred waters wash away uncleanliness, so doth thy merciful goodness cleanse the inward man: for the sacred stream in which mortals wash is for thy worship and thanksgiving.

9th verse. "Even he who sits by, and attends to thy words and worship, he also shall be fortunate; shall always have health, and shall live to a great age; and he shall see heaven.

10th verse. "O, thou who givest flame to fire! Reverence be to thee! for thou art most powerful: thou sendest rain to the earth to revive the wheat.

11th verse. "Fire shrinks before thee; for thou art first among the planets in the firmament.

12th verse. "Thou art the eyes of the universe; for by light, man and beast, fish, and all things in the world are made visible."

PLATE 21.

POOJA OF GUNESH.

In this worship vermillion (sindoor), red sandal, raw rice, koosgrass, red flowers, bale-leaves, areka-nuts, betel-leaves, and treacle, are presented. A string of red flowers is thrown round the neck of the image of Gunesh, which is of red stone, occasionally black, and of brass. The sign worn in this Pooja is this , drawn with red vermillion; and a necklace of the seeds of the lotus is worn round the neck.

Translation of the Pooja of Gunesh.

The Poorans, Shastra, and Tuntra, enjoin three forms of worship.

1st verse. "Gunesh has twelve titles—Soomookh[1], Ek-dunt[2], Kupil[3], Gujkurnika[4], Lumbodur[5], Baikrit[6], Bipudnas[7], Binayak[8], Dhoomraketoo[9], Balachundra[10], Gujanun[11], Gunadisha[12].

2d verse. "Whosoever shall worship thee in these twelve titles, and whosoever shall attend and hearken to these names, shall surely be prosperous in this world.

3d verse. "Whosoever shall repeat these twelve names on the day of marriage or birth, or on proceeding on a journey, on going to battle, or in sickness, and on entering a new habitation, shall surely be delivered from all the evils of this life.

4th verse. "O Bakratunda[*]! O Maha Kaya[†]! thy face is resplendent, like a thousand suns! O Deo, prosper all my undertakings!

5th verse. (Joining his hands, he says)—"O, thou bulky and low of stature, thine head is like the elephant's! Thine ambrosial breath attracts the winged insects of the air to hover about thy balmy lips. Thy tusk is so formidable, that thou slayest with one stroke the enemies of them that worship thee. Vermillion is upon thy brow. Thou art the adopted son of Devee; and thou art ever liberal in thy gifts.

6th verse. "Such art thou, Gunesh! behold, I bow to thee! for thou art beautiful, being yellow in colour; and thou hast three eyes.

7th verse. (Presenting the lighted artee in circular motion before the idol)—"Thou art corpulent; thou art the ruler of the universe; and thou art the adopted son of Parbuttee. O Deo, deliver us from evils! Deity, deliver us!

[1] The beautiful.
[2] Single-toothed.
[3] Red and yellow complexioned.
[4] Elephant-eared.
[5] Corpulent.
[6] Mis-shapen.
[7] Deliverer from evil.
[8] The leader.
[9] Smoke-bannered.
[10] Minor moon.
[11] Elephant-visaged.
[12] Chief of the bands of demigods.
[*] Elephant-trunked.
[†] Bulky-form.

8th verse. "Men prostrate themselves before thee, and worship thy feet, above all other works. Thy aliment is only of sweets; thou art borne by a mouse; and thy palace is splendour itself. O Deo, deliver us!

9th verse. "Thou bestowest wealth upon all those who worship thee; and thou fulfillest all their wishes. O Deo, help us! Deity, deliver us!

10th verse. "Thou art broad-browed. Thou wearest a necklace of crystal beads; and thou art the enemy of the evil one, and the friend and preserver of all those who worship thee. Deity, help us! Deity, help us!

11th verse. "Thou holdest the trident in thine hand; and thou hast been merciful unto me. Deity, help us! O Deo, deliver us!

12th verse. "The gods tremble before thee; and thou turnest thy arm to strike the demons. O Deo, help us! O Deo, deliver us!

13th verse. "O, thou first-worshipped, grant me wisdom and understanding; and cast out all wickedness and vanity from me, and make me holy. O Deity, help us! Deity, deliver us!

14th verse. "It is said that he who blows the shunk or the trumpet in thy praise, and presents the lighted artee in thy worship, shall have all his desires fulfilled. O Deo, help us! Deity, help us!

15th verse. "Those, who shall sing thy praise in the verses of Gunpati, shall surely prosper. Be gracious unto us! O Deo, help us! O Deo, help us!"

POOJA OF GUNESH.

PLATE 22.

POOJA TO HUNOOMAN.

HUNOOMAN was born on a Saturday, and took his seat, for the first time, in the Council of War on a Tuesday: on the same day he was first worshipped. The Brahmin, having terminated his devotions, repeats the Sundhya, and one thousand verses of the Gayatri: he bathes the Idol; and mixing up some vermilion and ghee, he smears the image all over with it: then places before it his offering of rice, sweetmeats, boiled gram, cocoa-nut, bale-leaves, red flowers, chikor-leaves, dhoopghass (hay), betel-leaves, and arecka-nuts. A small cake of flour and treacle is placed in the bottom of a kutora, over which the Devotee pours water from an abkhora with a brass spoon. The lighted artee, and all brass vessels, as in the other Poojas. He then joins his hands, and repeats the following

TRANSLATION OF THE POOJA OF HUNOOMAN.

1st verse. "Thou art swifter in thy movements than thought; and thou out-runnest the winds! Thou art wiser than wisdom itself; and thou ravishest all our senses! Thou art born of the winds; and thou art the king of the monkeys, and the favourite of Rama! Such art thou, O Hunooman! Reverence be to thee!

2d verse. "Thou hast not thy equal in this world for strength! Thy body shineth like burnished gold! Thou canst burn the Daityas to ashes: and thou art superior in all knowledge and wisdom.

3d verse. "Reverence to thee, O Hunooman! Deliver me from the power of evil-workers and evil-thinkers; and from the power of necromancers deliver me! Deliver me!

4th verse. "Preserve me from sickness, want, and all the evils of this life. Deliver me! Deliver me!

5th verse. "O thou of five faces! Ram Chunder is thy god, and Unjunee is thy mother! Preserve me!"

The worshipper here makes the signs with his fingers of the Unga-nyás, as repeated in the Sundhya; then the Hridayadinyas: then closing his eyes, and folding his arms, he repeats the following:—

6th verse. "O son of Unjunee and Vayoo, the god of the winds! Thy strength is great, above all things in nature! Thou art the deliverer of Seeta. Thou art the destroyer of Lunka. Thou art the friend of Urjoon. Thy voice is so powerful, that it resounds throughout the universe; and thou canst leap over seven seas: thine eyes are yellow: thou worshippest the sun! Thou art the preserver of Ungud, Lukshmun, and the monkey-army. Thou art the defeater of Rawan; and thou givest delight to Rama and Seeta. One of thy visages is black: it looks towards the east. The one to the south is yellow; the western one is red; thy northern one is green; and thy fifth face looks up to heaven: is white!

PLATE 22

POOJA OF HUNOOMAN

PLATE 23.

PUNCH AGNEE (PENANCE BY THE HEAT OF FIVE FIRES).

THIS is among the various penances performed by the Hindoo Devotees, annually during the three hottest months, April, May, and June. Within a square space, of about 2½ or 3 feet, he seats himself upon a small mat, cross-legged, as illustrated in this Plate, with the Pooran in his hand, which he continues to read during three hours, retaining the same posture immovably the whole time, whilst the fierce rays of the mid-day sun dart upon his bare head. Four fires, consisting of as many piles of dried cow-dung (commonly called *Kund*), and placed in the four corners of the mat, are kept up in full blaze. These fires produce a very ardent flame, and, consequently, an almost insupportable heat. The penitent does not shave during the whole of this probationary period, viz. three months. "Punch Agnee" signifies "Five Fires:" the Sun, above the head of the Devotee, is considered the fifth.

PLATE 23

PUNCH AGNEE

PLATE 24.

MARKS WORN BY THE BRAHMINS.

The high caste of Brahmins, who officiate as High Priests in the Temples of the Devtas, follow strictly and minutely every article enjoined by their Shastres and Poorans. The marks worn by them are only six, as illustrated in the annexed Plate. The ornaments, likewise, appertain to the Pooja of each particular Deity. The marks worn by the Brahmins being distinct and few, they evidently demonstrate what Divinity he has worshipped on that day; but the other castes, such as Chuttree, Byse, and Kaiyat, have marks so varied and numerous, each according to the whim or fancy of the wearer, that it is very difficult to trace what Divinity he has worshipped on that day, being a complication of signs appertaining to the worship of two or three different Gods, or Saints, at the same time. The Jogees, especially, are covered, all over the body, with various signs, drawn with white sandal, or simply with river-mud; sometimes with vermilion, or with black and yellow earth; all of which contribute not a little to their hideous, as well as grotesque appearance. The marks enjoined by their Shastres are four in number: these are put on immediately after ablution, by the four respective castes; viz. the Brahmin wears it thus ▯, perpendicularly on the forehead, between the brows, marked with white sandal or earth; the Chutriyas thus ☰, horizontally across the forehead, with the same; the Byse thus U, erect in front of the forehead; the Soodra, a round white spot, as large as a shilling-piece, between the eyebrows. These are worn during the performance of the Sundhya, and are washed off, to be replaced by those appertaining to the Deity the votary intends worshipping that day.

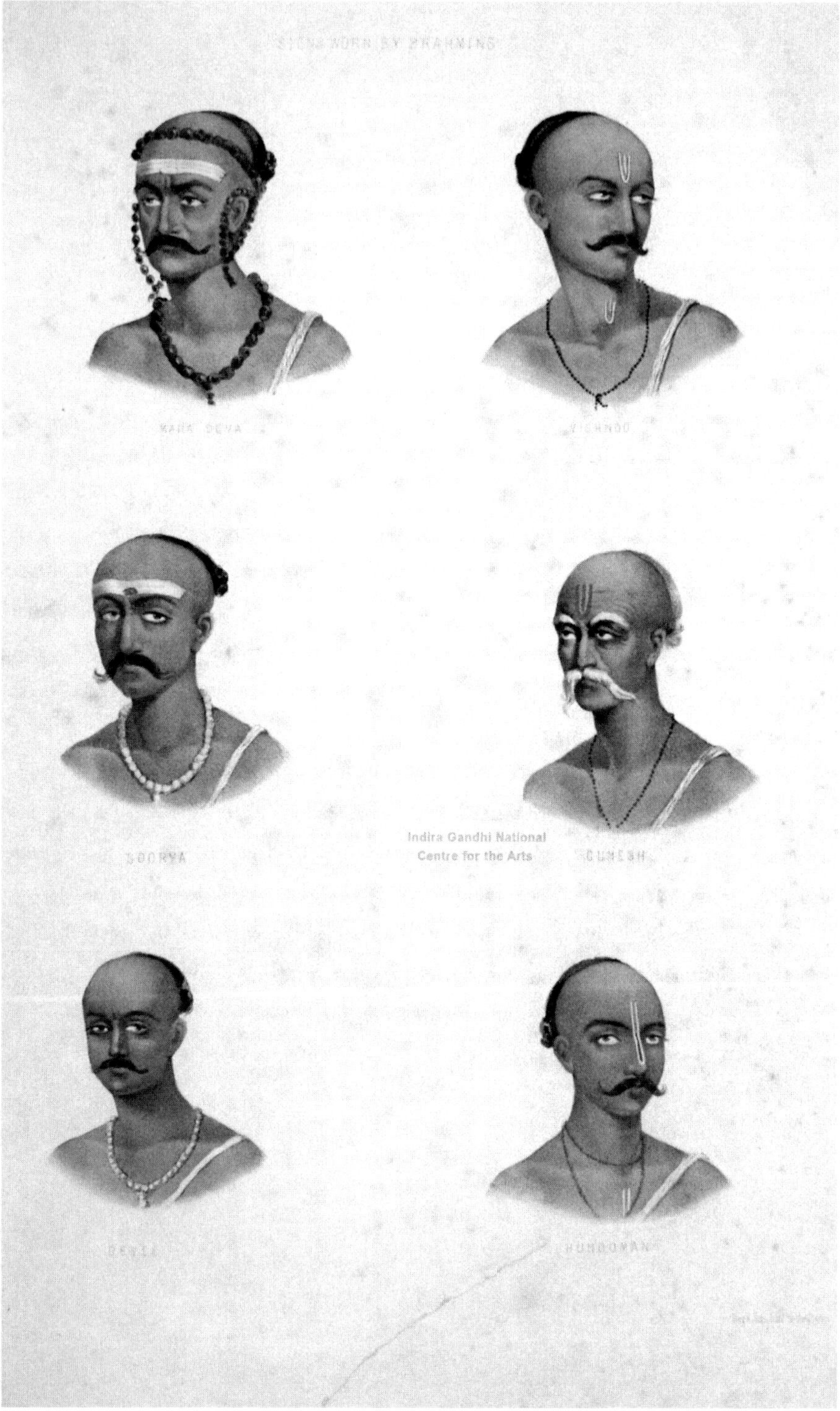
SIGNS WORN BY BRAHMINS
MAHA DEVA
VISHNOO
SOORYA
GUNESH
HUNOOMAN